FANTASTIC SPORTS FACTS

ICE HOCKEY

Michael Hurley

Raintree

Chicago, Illinois

Edited by Catherine Veitch, Sian Smith, and John-Paul Wilkins
Designed by Richard Parker
Picture research by Tracy Cummins
Originated by Capstone Global Library Ltd
Printed and bound in China

16 15 14 13 12
10 9 8 7 6 5 4 3 2 1

Library of Congress Cataloging-in-Publication Data
Cataloging-in-Publication data is available at the Library of Congress.
ISBN 978-1-4109-5106-9 (hbk)
ISBN 978-1-4109-5113-7 (pbk)

Acknowledgments
The author and publisher are grateful to the following for permission to reproduce copyright material: Alamy p. 9 (© Gunter Marx); Getty Images pp. 10 (Allsport), 13 (David Dow/NHLI), 14 (NHLI), 17 (Bruce Bennett Studios), 18 (Focus On Sport), 21 (Leon Halip), 22 (Francois Lacasse/ NHLI), 23 (John Tlumacki/The Boston Globe), 24 (Jim Leary), 25, 26, 27 (Bruce Bennett Studios); Library of Congress Prints and Photographs p. 7; Newscom pp. 11 (Will Schneekloth/Icon SMI CEU), 12, 15 (EPA/ JEFF KOWALSKY), 20 (Mark Welsh/ Rapport Press); Shutterstock pp. 4, 16 (© Patrick Tuohy), 5 (© fstockfoto), 8 left (© AlexTois), 8 right (© Igor Sokolov), 9 top (© nikkytok), 19 (© muzsy); www.puckedinthehead.com p. 6 (© Jason Kurylo).

Cover photograph of Hayley Wickenheiser of Canada controlling the puck during the women's ice hockey semi-finals game against Finland on Day 7 of the Turin 2006 Winter Olympic Games on February 17, 2006 at the Palasport Olimpico in Turin, Italy, reproduced with permission of Getty Images (Al Bello), and a hockey puck reproduced with permission of istockphoto (© nicole waring).

Every effort has been made to contact copyright holders of any material reproduced in this book. Any omissions will be rectified in subsequent printings if notice is given to the publisher.

All the Internet addresses (URLs) given in this book were valid at the time of going to press. However, due to the dynamic nature of the Internet, some addresses may have changed, or sites may have changed or ceased to exist since publication. While the author and publisher regret any inconvenience this may cause readers, no responsibility for any such changes can be accepted by either the author or the publisher.

Contents

Some words are printed in bold, **like this**. You can find out what they mean by looking in the glossary.

Hockey Basics

The NHL is based in the United States and Canada.

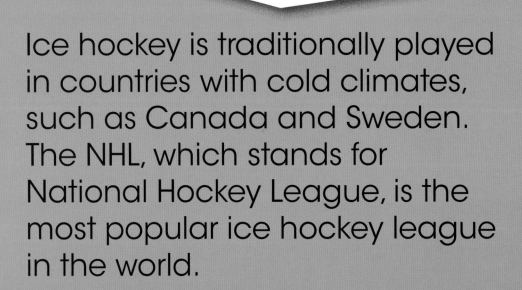

Ice hockey is traditionally played in countries with cold climates, such as Canada and Sweden. The NHL, which stands for National Hockey League, is the most popular ice hockey league in the world.

Hockey is one of the most popular sports at the Winter Olympics.

Longest Game

The longest game in history took place in Burnaby, Canada, in 2011. Two teams played hockey for 243 hours in a row. That is more than 10 days! The players were raising money for charity.

DID YOU KNOW?

The longest NHL game in history was between the Detroit Red Wings and the Montreal Maroons in 1936. The game lasted 116 minutes and 30 seconds, and ran into the sixth **overtime** period!

The Detroit Olympia was home of the Red Wings until 1979. It was nicknamed "The Old Red Barn."

Largest Stick and Puck

The largest hockey stick and puck in the world can be found in Vancouver, Canada. They were built in 1985 as part of a huge **exhibition** that drew people to the area.

DID YOU KNOW?

Hockey pucks are made out of **vulcanized rubber.** It is the same material that car tires are made from.

The largest hockey stick is 40 times bigger than a normal one!

Winners and Losers

The record for the longest winning streak in the history of the NHL is 17 games. This record was set during the 1992–1993 season by the Pittsburgh Penguins.

11

The Stanley Cup

The Stanley Cup is the trophy awarded to the winners of the NHL each season. It was first presented in 1893. It is one of the largest trophies in professional sports!

Each player on the winning team is given some time to keep the cup at home.

DID YOU KNOW?

The Stanley Cup has grown in size over the years. Each time the winning team and names of its players were added to it, a new section was added to the bottom of the trophy.

It's Raining Rats!

During the Stanley Cup finals in 1996 between the Florida Panthers and Colorado Avalanche, it started raining rats inside the stadium. Every time the Panthers scored, their fans would throw plastic rats onto the ice!

FUN FACT

Fans of the Detroit Red Wings like to throw an octopus onto the ice during the **playoffs**. This has seemed to bring the Red Wings good luck.

Fighting on the Ice

Fighting has always been a part of ice hockey. The sport is well known for the players getting in fights during a game.

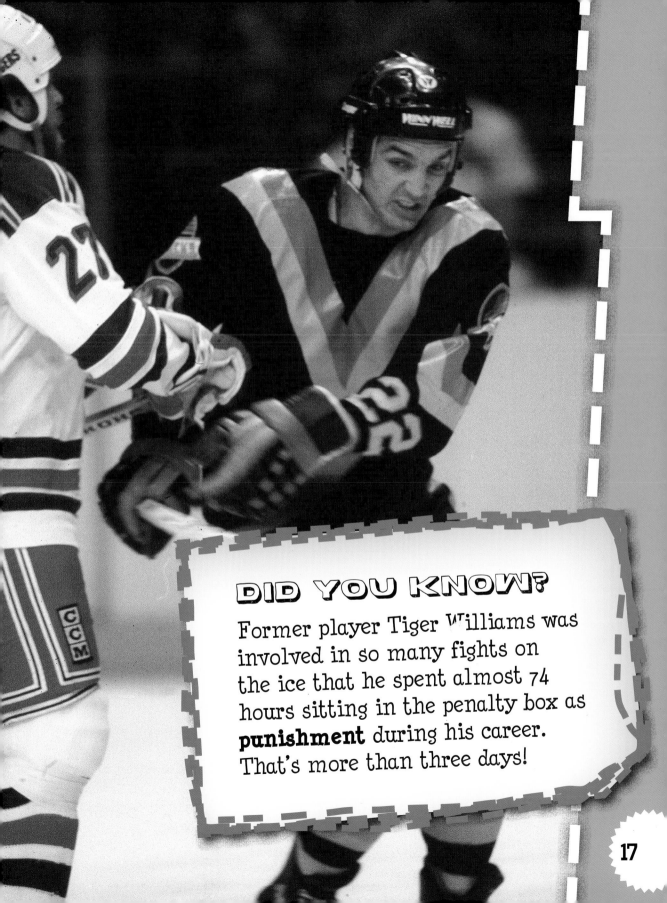

DID YOU KNOW?

Former player Tiger Williams was involved in so many fights on the ice that he spent almost 74 hours sitting in the penalty box as **punishment** during his career. That's more than three days!

Hockey Equipment

It wasn't until 1979 that helmets for new NHL players became part of the rules. Up until then, it was the choice of the players whether they wore a helmet or not.

Today, players wear lots of padding to prevent injury. Hockey players are very **agile**, and move quickly over the ice, despite all of the padding.

helmet

glove

knee pad

skate

Huge Crowds

Sometimes there are so many fans that they build ice rinks in bigger sports stadiums! A huge crowd filled the Wrigley Field baseball stadium for an NHL game between the Chicago Blackhawks and Detroit Red Wings in 2009.

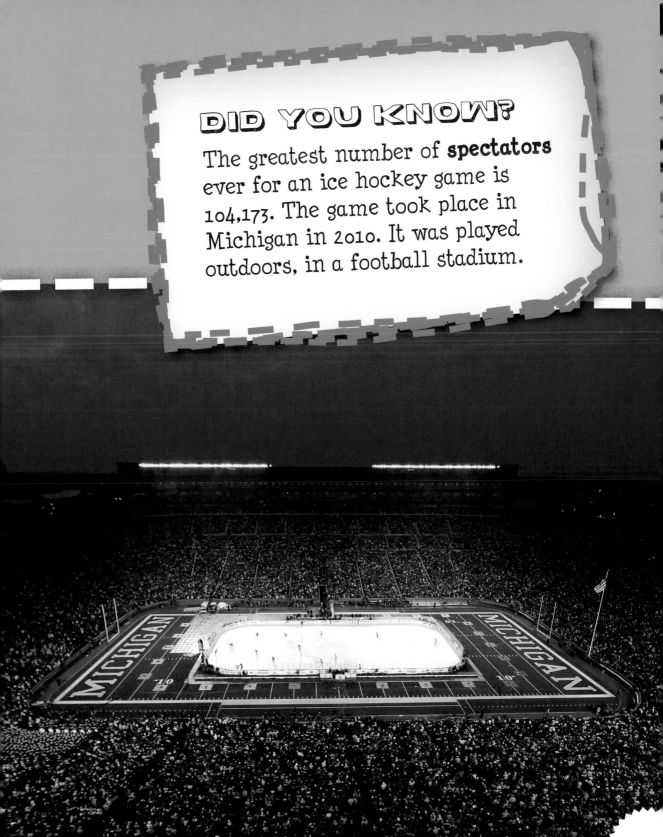

DID YOU KNOW?

The greatest number of **spectators** ever for an ice hockey game is 104,173. The game took place in Michigan in 2010. It was played outdoors, in a football stadium.

Highest-Scoring Games

There have been an incredible 21 goals scored twice in NHL games. The first time was in 1920, when the Montreal Canadiens beat the Toronto St. Patricks 14–7. In 1985, the Edmonton Oilers beat the Chicago Blackhawks 12–9.

Hockey fans love to see the puck hitting the back of the net!

DID YOU KNOW?

The most goals scored by one team in a game is 16. The Montreal Canadiens beat the Quebec Bulldogs 16-3.

Great Players

The most famous player in the history of ice hockey is Wayne Gretzky. He was born in Canada and played in the NHL for 21 years. Gretzky was given the nickname "The Great One."

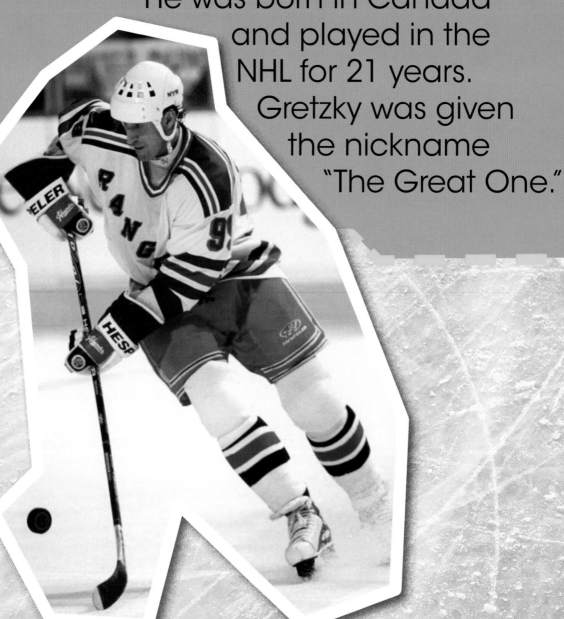

Wayne Gretzky helped the Edmonton Oilers win the Stanley Cup four times.

DID YOU KNOW?

Gretzky holds, or shares, an amazing 61 NHL records. This includes the record for most goals and most **assists**.

One of the greatest female ice hockey players is Canada's Hayley Wickenheiser. She was first picked to play for her country in the Olympics when she was just 15 years old!

DID YOU KNOW?

As part of the Canadian women's team, Wickenheiser has won three gold medals and one silver medal at the Winter Olympics.

Quiz

Are you a superfan or a couch potato? Decide whether the statements below are true or false. Then look at the answers on page 31 and check your score on the fanometer.

1 Ice hockey pucks are made from the same material as car tires.

2 Canada has won more Olympic Gold medals for ice hockey than any other country.

3 The Edmonton Oilers have won the Stanley Cup the most times.

TOP TIP
Some of the answers can be found in this book, but you may have to find some yourself.

4 Wayne Gretzky is known as "The Great One."

5 Detroit Red Wings fans throw a squid onto the ice to give their team good luck.

6 Hayley Wickenheiser was picked for the Olympic team at 17 years old.

FANOMETER

couch potato

fair-weather fan

superfan

1   **2**   **3**   **4**   **5**   **6**

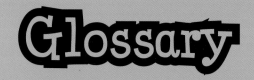

Glossary

agile able to move quickly and easily

assist pass that enables the player who receives it to score a goal

exhibition collection of things put on display for people to look at

playoffs end-of-season series of games to see who becomes the overall champion

punishment way of making someone suffer for doing something wrong

spectators group of people who watch a game or show

vulcanized rubber rubber that has been treated to make it stronger and more durable

Find Out More

Books

Biskup, Agnieszka. *Ice Hockey: How it Works* (The Science of Sport). Chicago: Raintree, 2012.

Johnson, Robin. *Ice Hockey and Curling* (Winter Olympic Sports). New York: Crabtree Publishing, 2009.

Web sites

Facthound offers a safe, fun way to find Internet sites related to this book. All of the sites on Facthound have been researched by our staff.

Here's all you do:

Visit www.facthound.com

Type in this code: 9781410951069

Quiz answers

1) True (see page 9).
2) True.
3) False. The Montreal Canadiens have won the most Stanley Cups, with 23.
4) True (see page 24).
5) False. The Detroit Red Wings fans throw an octopus onto the ice for good luck (see page 15).
6) False. Wickenheiser was just 15 years old when she was picked for the Olympic team (see page 26).

Index